From the Streets to the Sanctuary

GERRI ROSIECKI

From the Streets to the Sanctuary

Copyright © 2024 by Gerri Rosiecki

Printed in the United States of America First Printing, 2024

ISBN: 979-8-9892300-2-0

Leftwich Press, Inc.
Brooklyn, NY
www.LeftwichPressChristianPublishing.com

DEDICATION

I dedicate this book to my husband, Joe Rosiecki, Sr. Thank you for always being there for me, never leaving me, and always supporting and funding everything I have chosen to set out to do. Thank you because even when others questioned why you ever got with me, you never wavered from your God-given assignment: ME.

ACKNOWLEDGMENTS

First, I want to thank my Heavenly Father because I would not be here to tell the testimony without him.

I want to thank my children for everything we have shared, laughed at, and embraced together; as long as God is on the throne, I declare you will reach your God-given potential.

Thank you to my Pastor and First Lady, Bishop Christopher J. Hodge, and Lady Karen Hodge, for loving and embracing me just for who I am, for always encouraging me, and for giving me spiritual spankings because that is what parents do. And to my NDT family, thank you.

To Mother Sumner, I love how you love me and my family. You are the true definition of a church Mother.

To Deacon and Minister Mann, you accepted me for who I was the first time you met me, and you guys have remained the same, blessed, and highly favored.

Mama and Papa Hodge, thank you for never leaving my side.

Last but not least, Elder Iris Rose, you are and always will be a blessing to me. You have always been there every time I called, and I thank God for you. You are a rock in my life.

CONTENTS

FOREWORD

Many years ago, I was graced to meet a most remarkable young lady. What I saw was her sincerity. She was a true believer and worshiper of God. There was no pretense, and she was exactly what you saw. She can see herself from the past to the present and then talk about it to help others.

Gerri preaches wherever you see her and expresses her gratitude to God daily. The town she grew up in is filled with many who need to hear a word from the Lord, and because of Gerri, they hear that word. Knowing from whence she has come makes her words much more powerful.

When I go to her town with her, she preaches to any who wishes to hear the Word of God, whether she knows them or not. We spent a day together, and the number of random people she asked if she could pray for them was astounding. She also asked people with babies and children if she could pray for them. What is so remarkable about Gerri is her willingness to share the gospel of Jesus Christ and her sincerity. Often, she says I am not perfect, but if I can help somebody along the way, I will help them.

People often say I cannot find a job, but not Gerri. She will leave her job today and get three jobs tomorrow. Using the mantra of Alcoholics Anonymous, "Keep coming back works." Gerri is a wonderful example of the truth of that exact statement.

Her Christianity is visible to anyone she encounters. She is a prime example of "go out and preach the word."

Sincerity personified is what I think of Gerri.

Gerri is married to a highly committed and supportive husband.

God bless and continue to keep all who believe there is no hope. There is always hope if you are willing to do your part. God is always there, just waiting for you to come to him.

Patricia Sumner, BS, RN, CARN

1
INTRODUCTION

I cannot believe I am back here again.

That place is one that I said I would never return to.

You know when you have been doing so good, you forget the things God has delivered you from?

Well… that is what happened to me.

Oh, my goodness. I shared my experience, strength, and hope with people. My unadulterated testimony until I gave so much of myself that I lost myself. The Bible says it best to take heed lest you fall. "Wherefore let him that thinketh he standeth take heed lest he fall." I Corinthians 10:12 (KJV)

I drank alcohol again.

Whew!

It started as having a casual drink only at the family cookouts once a month. Then it turned to twice a month, and eventually, I began drinking every weekend. And when I drank, I drank. Because my family can drink responsibly, I forgot what God had delivered me from...

ME.

2
IN THE BEGINNING

I am Gerri Rosiecki, originally Gerri Saunders, born on March 22, 1967, in Newburgh, New York, at St. Luke's Hospital. Memories began to form around age three when my sister and I found ourselves in the care of the Hall family as foster children. I distinctly recall the casual exchange between Mrs. Moore, our social worker, and Mrs. Hall regarding a pile of dirty diapers on the back porch.

As I lounged on their couch, enjoying a crisp apple, I could not help but admire the elegant wood-paneled walls and the glass pocket door that divided the living and dining areas. Despite the sorrow of Mrs. Hall's passing before our adoption was finalized, Mr. Hall courageously took on the role of a single parent, becoming our steadfast father figure from that point onward.

The Hall household was lively, always bustling with foster kids and overflowing with love. Set in a picturesque Craftsman-style home, it exuded warmth and comfort from every nook and cranny. Our Sundays were for church. We worshipped at Ebenezer Baptist Church in Newburgh, NY, where Mrs. Hall sang in the choir. To keep me quiet during service, she would slip me a couple of Tums—a sly trick that worked like a charm.

One Christmas stands out vividly in my memory. The sheer number of presents overflowed from beneath the tree, spilling into the foyer—a testament to the generosity and warmth that filled our home. No wonder I have always had a soft spot for big families; the sense of belonging and abundance was there.

When Mrs. Hall passed away, things changed. While other foster kids found new homes, my sister and I remained with our dad, who embraced single parenthood with open arms. Despite the challenges, his love and support never wavered, and his extended family stepped up to lend a hand.

Digging into my roots, I found my birth certificate, revealing my original name as Gerri Lyn Saunders. My biological dad, Eddie Saunders Jr., hailed from Poughkeepsie, NY, while my mom, Jaclyn Saunders, had roots in Highland Falls, NY. Her maiden name was Hargrove. I had the pleasure of meeting my maternal grandfather, great-grandmother, and paternal grandfather. It was a profound experience that filled in some of the missing pieces of my identity. I had a beautiful relationship with my grandfather.

Mr. Hall would allow him to pick up my sister and me on the weekends so we could stay with him in Poughkeepsie. These were cherished moments, filled with trips to the Dutchess County Fair during the summertime. He also helped us with our school supplies during the year. During these visits, my fondness for wrestling, particularly the televised bouts of the seventies, took root—Jimmy, better known as SuperFly Snuka, quickly became my favorite wrestler.

My grandfather was a colorful character in his own right. He was not fond of his son, my biological father. We would drive past my biological father on his motorcycle, and my grandfather would say, "There's your father." My biological father had one arm. I later learned that one of the girlfriends he used to beat had shot it off. I heard stories of how he was abusive to my mom and shook one of my little sisters to death. All I could think was, "I guess he's not beating up women now with one arm." Thank God my mother left him because that could have been me or my sister.

And I thank God for the Hall family. They helped to save our lives.

3
GROWING UP

Everything happens for a reason. Growing up in the Hall household led me to church, which led me to know who God was. I learned to serve the Lord at an early age and have a reverence for God. I served on the Junior Usher Board, Sunday School Choir, Junior Nursing Board, and Vacation Bible School. I even started teaching the little ones in Sunday School when I was eleven.

Our Sunday School program was well put together. We put on Easter and Christmas plays. Every Christmas, each child received a gift and a money envelope with $5. We had a 4H Club, and by the way, I was the president for two years. I was always eager to help and serve, not for man, but for God. They took us to Great Adventure, Rye Playland, and the Midnight Ride to Coney Island every summer. When I served on the Youth Choir, we went to sing at other churches and would even go as far as New York City.

Before I move on to my teenage years, I must let you know what happened to me when I was eight. It was devasting. My dad started dating a mean, nasty, and vindictive lady from Brooklyn who had two teenagers. This woman was nothing like his previous girlfriend, who was a sweetie pie and was not anything like Mrs. Hall. When she moved in and they got married, everything changed. She beat me, and her son sodomized me. He would rape me in the bathroom.

Her daughter locked me in the closet and molested me. This was the family from hell. I was so grateful and happy that this marriage did not last. They did not go without a fight, but they left. Once they were out of our lives, everything became normal again. And when I say normal, I mean we were a family again. My dad, sister, and I began going on vacations south to Batesville, Mississippi, Tennessee, and Chicago. It is incredible how I can remember those bad and good days in my younger years. Even then, God sustained my mind and had a plan and a purpose for my life. I could have lost my mind during those years; however, God sustained me.

4
SCHOOL DAYS

My sister and I attended Saint Francis Catholic School. We were the only Black people when we started. The bus rides home from school were rough in the beginning, but as we got older, the white kids started to accept us. I started loving basketball in Saint Francis. When my dad finally let me go to public school, it was like someone let me out of a cage. I attended Meadow Hill Public School; it was sixth grade. I sharpened my basketball skills there.

I went to Meadow Hill for 6th and 8th grades. My dad put me back in private school for seventh grade. My sister and I convinced him to go to public school for eighth grade, so my sister went with me. We had so much fun! I made a lot of friends, and my grades even improved. I feel the nuns at the private school did not allow me to reach my potential. We made many friends from Newburgh, even the kids who went to church with us, shouting out Delcina, Twinkle, and Skittle. We also had friends from the neighborhood, Tonya (Monk) and Hundy. Meadow Hill, North Junior High School, and Newburg Free Academy (NFA) are where I developed and understood who I was. I also began to like boys during this time.

Unfortunately, there was an incident with a male gym teacher from Meadow Hill School. I was in the girls' locker room. This teacher came into the locker room, grabbed me, and stuck his tongue down my throat. It never went any further, and I never told anyone. I do not know why I did not tell anyone. I should have told someone.

I will sum up my days at North Junior High as very adventurous, and thankfully, my basketball skills increased and developed. I became an outstanding basketball player. I traveled with the basketball team when I got to Newburg Free Academy. All the kids at NFA were in one building, so I got to know many people. High School was both exciting and sad. So many things transpired during those years. I began smoking marijuana in high school. In 10th grade, I got pregnant. I had an abortion, but my dad disapproved of it. In 11th grade, at the height of my basketball season, my dad passed away; I was 16 years old.

His death still bothers me. I spoke words that I deeply regret because I know that the power of life and death is in the tongue. I wanted to be grown and leave my dad's house. Of course, he said "no." I remember saying, "I wish he would die." One month later, he passed. It was as if all sense of security was gone. By this time, my father had married again; my stepmom was decent. The house seemed dark after his passing.

I drank and smoked marijuana daily. However, one thing I did was go to school every day. I got up and went to school; I did not need anyone to tell me to get up and go to school. I went to school the morning my dad died. As I look back now, I was indeed in shock. I had decided I was grown and on my own.

One thing I regret is not continuing to go to church. I thank God the word declares, train a child in the way he should go; when he is older, he will not depart from it. As I began my growth journey during this time, I thanked God for my relationship with my Heavenly Father. I stayed out late but made it to school. Home life was getting rough. I would argue with my stepmother daily. She was angry and had her issues because my dad left my sister and me everything, including the house and insurance policies. She kept trying to get her lawyer to put me in a group home, but they told her that as long as I was going to school, there was nothing they could do. She tried to get me out of the house, but I told her, "It's my house!"

Nobody could legally do anything until I turned eighteen. I remained in the house with my stepmother and received social security checks for my parents' deaths. I also had a job working at my cousin's record shop. My aunt would buy me clothes, and this is how I survived financially.

We finally had the will read on my birthday, March 22, 1985. Because my dad left her nothing, we divided things up three ways. We had to sell the house and move in with my aunt. I had the freedom to do whatever I wanted.

I continued to work at my cousin's record shop in my senior year of high school. I was not playing basketball anymore due to a fractured ankle. My boyfriend, whom I had been with since 10th grade, was a leech and just hung around me. He was a local DJ, and I bought him some equipment. I paid for our entire prom, including his tuxedo. While hanging around with my cousin at the record shop, I watched my cousin flip money by promoting rap concerts. I met RUN DMC, The Fat Boys, and Whodini. I even rode in the limousines with them. I was a local social light in Newburgh.

After prom and graduation, I took a week-long trip to Chicago to visit my father's brother, Uncle Robert, who was the executor of my father's will. Uncle Robert wanted to see me and see how I was doing.

5
THE STREETS

When I returned to New York, I discovered my lame boyfriend was a cheater. He was messing with a few girls. I started sniffing coke and hanging out with some not-so-good people. A friend of mine introduced me to a significant coke dealer. We would get high and have sex. I started looking bad, and I moved in with my sister (she did not get high).

I sniffed so much coke one day that my nose bled. I was still working at my cousin's record shop. I blew through all my money. I left my sister's apartment because I did not want to get high at night under the same roof as my nephew. I moved across the street with a lady and her family; they rented me a room and helped me get back on my feet. I got a job at West Point Military Academy.

Soon, I was back working like a normal, productive member of society. I linked up with a girl from the school. We were young and pretty, and the cadets loved us. After about a year of doing good, my fast behind fell infatuated with the ugliest man on the planet. His face could stop the clock, but his body was banging. This was the beginning of the end, or so the devil thought. I started dating him, and my family warned me about him. He was a convicted felon who turned women out on drugs and prostitution, and the main thing was that he was a woman beater. But, when your flesh wants what it wants, and as my dad used to say, "a hard head makes a soft behind," the warnings kept coming, and I kept saying not me, and you reason with yourself and others.

Well, the devil is a liar. Well, not only was he still like that, but I was in for the fight of my life. He started out being a gentleman, then he made love to me and did things that were never done to me sexually. I was all in. He tried to hide his drug addiction to crack cocaine. I remember when a commercial would come on television about Crack, and I would get a nasty taste in my mouth and yell. That was my warning, but I did not take heed.

I caught him smoking one day at a house. I had been looking for him all day when I found him. He had the pipe in his hand, and I told him I would do it if he did not stop. And, of course, I picked up the pipe, but he did not even try to stop me. Like they say in Narcotics Anonymous, "they will get you high before you get them sober." I took my first hit, and my ear started ringing. I began talking up a storm, and the storm came.

I planned to take my next hit on my birthday. I was off to the races. It became more frequent. I could not work or function. He maintained a job because he was used to it; I turned to prostitution when he went to work. He never tried to pimp me; however, when he would catch me, he beat me to a pulp. He used to tell me that this was God's way of punishing him for pimping out all those white girls.

I used to have sex with men for free, so my logic said I might as well get paid to do it. I started tricking street dealers. Then a lady told me, "Girl, go down by the library to HOE STROLL. It is all that money down there and nice white men you can be with instead of messing with these guys for drugs. Get you some real cash." I met men from all social classes, and the money was good. In time, I left my man and was homeless for a while because the glass stem controlled me, also known on the streets as the Glass Dick. It became my pimp. Whenever it called me, I obeyed and did whatever I needed to get a hit.

These white men were married, single, crazy, and rich. When I could not get crack, or there were no ways of getting money, I would get the basing blues, which meant I would get depressed. During times like this, I would go to the emergency room and cry that I was "suicidal" so they could put me in a 2-week Psychiatric

Unit. That was my resting place, and I could regain some weight. But let me tell you something: mental illness is real. I genuinely believe bipolar disorder runs in my bloodline. And also, from the years of using drugs, I did do some damage to my brain.

I saw a lot of mental crises on the streets. Some people lost their minds on drugs; one young lady lost herself. Her mind was gone after her uncle raped her. He would chain her to a bed and let men sleep with her for drugs and money. I witnessed a baby about six months old left alone in an abandoned building while the mother went out to sell her body for crack. Thank God no child molester got wind of that. A friend of mine and I waited for the mother to come back, and I believe Child Protective Services picked the baby up. I also attempted suicide for real. I took a bunch of pills and tried to end it. I knew this was not the life I was supposed to have.

I got myself into a lot of trouble, stealing packages of drugs and stealing money. There were many good times, but when times were terrible, they were wrong. This is when I met the Gerri I thought I would never meet, and she did things I thought I would never do. I will not mention some of them because I must use discretion. But, to God be the glory. He is a keeper. It is only by His grace and mercy I do not have HIV or AIDS, herpes, or any of the like. He covered me.

My preference became white men because they paid well and finished quickly. No disrespect to my African American brothers, but I used to say "they want to take you around the world and back again for $5 and want change back." That was a little personal joke I used to tell myself. The winters were cold, snowy, and wet outside. I quickly learned to start drinking alcohol and became a runner or look out for some of the drug dealers (of course, that was to have high-quality rock), and getting high was so much better with it.

Hence, when loose rock came out, they stopped packaging it; I made my money, bought four cigarettes for $1, and spent $1 on cake, and juice, chips, and the rest went in my stem, or some days, I got two hot dogs for $1. I was happy and high with a full belly. I got hooked on alcohol quickly because at the age of five, I drank Johnny Walker whiskey straight and Grape Wine, so now I drank Thunderbird, all the old heads already know. I would take a big hit of crack and drink my wine, which I called the neutralizer. It brought me back to the level field. But, if I could not make any good money for crack and only had $1.70 for that bottle, oh boy, what a terror I was. I was Calamity Jane, for lack of better words.

The dealers would give me a crack rock to sober up or get lost. The last part was more correct…LOL. I would hang out with guys who had less drama. Plus, I was tomboyish anyway. And, when the customers, well Johns is what we called them, were in a shortage, the girl's true colors came out. I became obsessed with good-paying Johns because they treated and talked to me like a human. It was a time of escape with them from the madness and actual reality of what my life had become. Not only did they pay well, but they also tipped well.

I fell in love with one. I had seen him before, but he would not pick me up. But, oh, the day he did, I was hooked. He was beautiful and charming, and his voice was immaculate. I asked him if he ever played in a Soap Opera. He was that good-looking. He laughed and said, "No, I'm just a Joe Schmoe." He was very humble. He would come around once a week looking for a girl, and when he picked me up, we started creating a bond. I never pulled an Okie Doke on him. He was calm, gentle, and sweet—a Ying to my Yang.

6
REAL LOVE

The beautiful man with whom I was in love with was not a crack smoker. He liked to drink and smoke his weed when he got off work. He also had his own business. I remember the day I knew God destined him for me. It was 6 am, and I had a quickening in my spirit. My saints know what I am talking about; I was walking up the street, and the Holy Spirit said he was coming to town today. I ran to a friend's house, asked them if I could shower, and they gave me clean clothes. And, sure enough, later that day, he came driving through Newburgh. I knew of God and his power; I fell in love with God at seven and got baptized. I always had a genuine love for my Heavenly Father; I guess that is why, at the early age of eight and up, the devil would come for me through different family members. Thankfully, I had a powerful spirit of discernment in me, too.

This man became my husband. I already had three children when I met him, and he had none. Thank you, Jesus. The old, seasoned church mothers would use the phrase "an overnight turnaround." I know just what that is. I went from homeless to a home paid in full overnight. God did it just like that, and it was paid in full. I always knew that God favored me. I remember things that could have taken me out, like going to jail, overdosing, and more, BUT GOD stayed his hand.

When we moved into our home, I knew how to be domestic. That is one thing Daddy Hall taught us: we could not leave the house or play outside on Saturday mornings unless that house was clean. I have to mention that I got pregnant with my fourth child, who is my husband's child, before we moved into the house. I didn't raise her because I was running the streets. But my husband paid child support from her birth. She was placed with my third child, so they grew up together like my first and second child.

I got pregnant with my fifth child two years after we moved into our house. I kept him; I was good and off drugs for a while, but thank God my Boaz owned his own business, so he rearranged his schedule to care for our son. I do remember when I stole money from him, he put me out for two weeks. I was back on the streets again; what a way to teach someone a lesson. This experience genuinely humbled me. I had to go to the mission to ask for clothes since I left the house with no change of clothing. Boy, that spirit of addiction will have you doing things you do not want to do! You forget about EVERYTHING; there is no time to wash your behind or anything.

I was so grateful when he let me back in the house. I remember now what year it was. It was the only year there was no World Series. You know, it is funny how certain events trigger memories. I also left when our son was only two weeks old, running after crack. I came back two days later feeling guilty, as I should have. Boaz is a restorer.

Gerri Rosiecki

Joe & Gerri Rosiecki

7
THE SANCTUARY

Even through this, I kept my family in the church. After eight years of living together, we got married. One day, we were in church, and I said, "I do not want to be fornicating because we are living together unmarried." He looked at me and said, "Huh?" I told him if we did not get married, I would leave with Joe Jr. I did not want to disobey God. Thankfully, he married me swiftly. There are a lot of hurt and abandonment issues that we deal with, but we work through them.

As I aligned my life with God, one day, God put the Street Ministry in my spirit. I had to return to where he delivered me and let the people on the street know God had changed my life. When they saw me driving a Mercedes, they said my rich husband had done it. I had to tell them that it was God and Him alone. God will not share His glory with anyone. For years, I used to dream about my childhood home, and every time in the dream, I could not enter the house; either the pipes had burst, or something kept me from entering. Finally, after I dedicated my life to Christ, I walked down the street to my childhood home in my dream. I was allowed to enter. I woke up amazed that I had access. This dream resembled my life. As long as I was running the streets, smoking crack, selling my body away, and living a life away from God, I did not have access to life. I did not have access to a home for my soul. Giving my life to Christ was the best decision I have ever made.

Of course, I still face trials and temptations to this day. I had a short stint relapse of crack back in January 2019. Thankfully, it was short-lived. I went to my Pastor, laid my drugs on his desk, and told on myself. No one knew because I would dip in Newburgh, buy my drugs, and go home. God quickly snatched the taste of crack out of my mouth because that could have been tragic. It was the alcohol that took me a while to shake.

At the beginning of the book, I mentioned that I could not believe I was here again. After years of being off drugs, I thought I could casually drink. What a big lie that is. Knowing I am an alcoholic also, I felt with my bright ideas since I am sipping champagne, I can do this. LOL. I went from drinking at family cookouts once a month to every two weeks to every weekend. No one knew I was drinking, I told myself. See, the devil will hold you hostage physically, psychologically, and spiritually if you allow him to. I knew I would have lost my job, and if you want to keep it 100, I probably would have hit that pipe again if I hadn't made that move quickly.

Thank God for touching my mind. I woke up quickly and realized I could lose everything. I thank God I have a union job, and they gave me an FMLA to go to rehab.

I signed myself into rehab expeditiously, and for two weeks, I poured out into my recovery like never before. I used that as a time of consecration. I woke up every morning and read my Bible.

It was hard. I was so embarrassed I went on Zoom for Bible Study drunk and cutting up. Thank God my church family is supportive. My Bishop sent an anointed elder to see me. Shout out to Elder Iris Rose, who came with power and authority and busted the door to where I was. I can imagine the look on my face. I was so ashamed, but I thank God for good help. They got me a bed in the rehab I not only went to years earlier but also did my internship at. Man, that was a rude awakening, but I pushed through, and my experience, strength, hope, and faith were displayed for God's Glory.

I stay active in church, helping with the Cleaning Ministry. God is moving me in another direction this season. I continue to be a faithful member of New Day Tabernacle under the tutelage of Bishop Christopher J.

Hodge, the Apostle. I cannot mention him without mentioning his beautiful wife, Lady Karen Hodge. God has given me a church home where the Pastor is a true man of God, teacher, and disciplinarian; I am grateful for my life, health, and strength. God's hand has always been in my life. I did things that should have messed up, but God straightened it. He has kept me from dangers seen and unseen; he has given me a ministry for people, the very ones who hurt, despised, and falsely accused and abused me. I will still help them to a certain extent. I am maturing in every area of my life. I thank God for restoring me and keeping me from me. I am imperfect, but I keep pressing and reading my Bible. That is what is keeping me. As I look back on my life, I have a testimony. God has always been merciful and gracious to me.

The streets could have taken me out, but God's love is patient and enduring. He let me live, and I was able to get back to the sanctuary – to His house- so that I could live for Him. He does not shame or belittle me. God treats and loves me as his daughter. I am forever grateful to God that I survived the Streets to the Sanctuary.

www.ingramcontent.com/pod-product-compliance
Lightning Source LLC
Chambersburg PA
CBHW051713090426
42736CB00013B/2681